Computing
Workbook

1

Rebecca Franks, Dr Tracy Gardner and Liz Smart

William Collins' dream of knowledge for all began with the publication of his first book in 1819.

A self-educated mill worker, he not only enriched millions of lives, but also founded a flourishing publishing house. Today, staying true to this spirit, Collins books are packed with inspiration, innovation and practical expertise.

They place you at the centre of a world of possibility and give you exactly what you need to explore it.

Collins. Freedom to teach.

Published by Collins

An imprint of HarperCollins*Publishers*
The News Building, 1 London Bridge Street, London, SE1 9GF, UK

HarperCollins*Publishers*
Macken House, 39/40 Mayor Street Upper, Dublin 1, D01 C9W8, Ireland

Browse the complete Collins catalogue at
collins.co.uk

10 9 8 7 6 5 4 3 2 1

ISBN 978-0-00-868390-0

British Library Cataloguing-in-Publication Data

A catalogue record for this publication is available from the British Library.

Authors: Rebecca Franks, Dr Tracy Gardner and Liz Smart
Publisher: Catherine Martin
Product manager: Saaleh Patel
Project manager: Just Content Ltd
Development editor: Gemma Coleman
Copy editor: Tanya Solomons
Proofreader: Laura Connell
Cover designer: Gordon McGilp
Cover image: Amparo Barrera, Kneath Associates
Internal designer: Steve Evans, Planet Life Art
Illustration: Jouve India Ltd
Typesetter: Ken Vail Graphic Design
Production controller: Lyndsey Rogers
Printed and bound by Martins the Printers

This book contains FSC™ certified paper and other controlled sources to ensure responsible forest management.

For more information visit: harpercollins.co.uk/green

Acknowledgements

Support materials and screenshots are licensed under the Creative Commons Attribution-ShareAlike 2.0 license. We are grateful to the following for permission to reproduce screenshots. In some instances, we have been unable to trace the owners of copyright material, and we would appreciate any information that would enable us to do so.

Scratch Foundation: Authorised usage of screenshots showcasing Scratch programming environment elements.

Scratch is developed by the Lifelong Kindergarten Group at the MIT Media Lab: p.17–18, p.22–25, p.33–37, p.39, p.41. p.43, p.47.

Images

p.1 Den Rozhnovsky/Shutterstock, p.1 Lukas Gojda/ Shutterstock, p.1 Issarawat Tattong/Shutterstock, p.1 Miguel Lagoa/Shutterstock, p.1 vovan/Shutterstock, p.31 indigolotos/ Shutterstock, p.31 Anton Starikov/Shutterstock, p.31 Eakkapon Sriharun/Shutterstock, p.31 Voronin76/Shutterstock, p.31 Kamil Zajaczkowski/Shutterstock, p.32 indigolotos/Shutterstock, p.32 Studio_Fennel/Shutterstock, p.34 IVAN ROSHCHUPKIN/ Shutterstock, p.34 Issarawat Tattong/Shutterstock, p.34 Miguel Lagoa/Shutterstock, p.34 vovan/Shutterstock, p.34 indigolotos Shutterstock, p.34 Anton Starikov/Shutterstock, p.34 Eakkapon Sriharun/Shutterstock.

Contents

Introduction

In the Collins Stage 1 Computing Student's Book and Workbook you will find lots of fun and interesting activities and projects, which will help you develop your Computing skills.

There are Workbook tasks for every lesson in the Student's Book. Look for the references to the Workbook tasks on the Student's Book pages. Your teacher will tell you which tasks to do.

Each task will help you with the work you are doing in the Student's Book. This could be exercises to practise what you are learning about, or drawing and writing notes about your designs for your end of chapter projects.

In the reflection tasks you have the chance to think about a lesson or skill you have been practising. You can share these thoughts with the class or keep them private between you and your teacher.

We hope you enjoy learning about Computing in a practical and fun way!

Rebecca Franks, Dr Tracy Gardner and Liz Smart

Chapter 1: Our digital world

◐ Project: Design a robot to help someone who works at your school

---

| Chapter 1.1 | Computers around you |

Task A: Which is not a computer?

1 Circle the image that is not a computer.

Key terms

- **computer** – electronic machine that can perform tasks
- **app (program)** – used for specific tasks on a computer

desktop

tablet

E-reader

hardback book

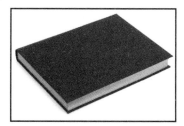

2 Circle the images that are not computers.

smartphone

laptop

games console

building blocks

school bag

 Return to Page 2 of the Student's Book.

1

Task B: I use a computer to...

Draw a picture to show how you like to use a computer.

Return to Page 3 of the Student's Book.

Task A: Digital devices and robots around you

Your teacher will now take you on a tour, or you will use the picture below.

Key terms

- **digital device** – object that contains a small computer to perform tasks
- **robot** – digital device that performs a useful task on its own; a robot may be able to move or talk

1 How many digital devices and robots can you find?

digital devices											
robots											

2 Draw the digital devices and robots that you find.

Return to Page 5 of the Student's Book.

Task A: The interview

1 Who are you interviewing? Write the name of your guest.

....

2 Write words to help you remember the tasks your guest tells you about.

....

....

....

....

....

....

....

....

....

....

....

....

....

....

....

....

3 Draw pictures to help you remember the tasks your guest tells you about.

Return to Page 7 of the Student's Book.

Task A: Choose a task to help your guest with

What task will your robot help your guest with?

....

....

....

2 Draw a picture to show how your task is completed at the moment.

Return to Page 9 of the Student's Book.

Task A: Sketch your robot ideas

1 Sketch some designs for your robot in this box.

Task B: Draw your final design

Tip Add labels and arrows to your robot to say what it is doing.

1 Draw and colour your final design.

2 What task will your robot help with?

....

....

....

 Return to Page 10 of the Student's Book.

Key terms

- **showcase** – present a project to an audience

Task A: Reflection

Tip Reflecting helps you to remember what you have learned.

1 How well would your robot help your guest? Colour the stars.

2 How well did you perform the showcase of your design? Colour the stars.

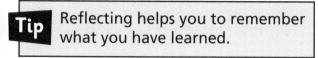 Return to Page 11 of the Student's Book.

Chapter 2: Content creation

● Project: Design and build an app that feeds a character their favourite foods

Chapter 2.1 | **Passwords**

Task A: Three random pictures

1 Draw **three** pictures that you could use to help you remember a pretend password that has three words.

Picture 1
Picture 2
Picture 3

Key terms

- **password** – secret code you use to keep your information safe
- **log on** – entering a username and password to use a computer
- **username** – personal name you use to access your information, for example to use a computer at school
- **log off** – exiting a computer when you have finished using it

Tip Don't write the word 'password' next to your three pictures. This will help to keep your password secret!

Return to Page 14 of the Student's Book.

Task B: Key terms practice

1 Trace the key terms with your pencil.

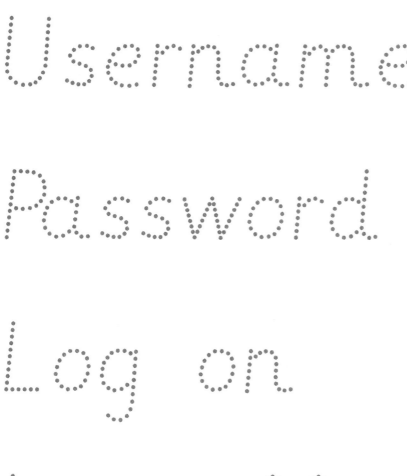

Username

Password

Log on

Log off

 Return to Page 15 of the Student's Book.

13

Task A: Choose three foods

1 Circle the **three** foods that you would like to use in your app.

Key terms

- **capital letters** – big letters that we use at the start of a sentence or a name. Capital letters are bigger than lowercase letters.
- **lowercase letters** – smaller letters that we use most of the time when we write and type. Lowercase letters are smaller than capital letters.

Return to Page 16 of the Student's Book.

Task B: Write your food words

Here are the ten foods that you can choose from with their names.

Taco

Melon

Muffin

Strawberry   Honey

Orange

Jam

Donut

Apple

Banana

◀ Write the names of your three chosen foods below.

Food 1: ....

Food 2: ....

Food 3: ....

Tip	Remember to use a capital letter at the start of each word.

Return to Page 17 of the Student's Book.

Task A: Find the capital letters

1 Circle all the capital letters. There are ten. The first one has been circled for you.

a (A) e i L K

k P n N J

g H h U u

Q q B b

Return to Page 19 of the Student's Book.

Task A: Scratch quiz

1 Which area of Scratch do you see in the picture below? Circle the answer.

Editor   **Stage**   **Sprites**

2 Can sprites have lots of costumes? Circle the answer.

Yes   **No**

3 How many sprites are in this picture?

Key terms

- **Scratch** – program that allows you to create your own programs or apps
- **open** – view a file on a computer
- **save** – save a file on a computer so that you can use it again next time
- **sprite** – character or object in Scratch
- **stage** – area in Scratch where you can play with your app
- **costume** – different options for how your sprite looks in Scratch. It is like the clothes you wear each day!

Return to Page 22 of the Student's Book.

Task A: Rate your progress

You have now played with your 'Feed Frank' app.

Rate your skills by colouring the pictures.

1 I can find the green flag to play my game.

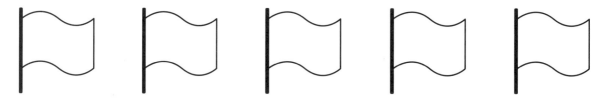

2 I can type my three foods.

3 I can use caps lock to type a capital letter.

4 I can drag and drop the food to feed Frank.

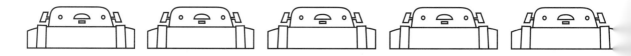

 Return to Page 24 of the Student's Book.

Task A: Reflection

1 How easy was it to create your Feed Frank app? Colour the stars.

2 How much fun did your audience have when playing your game? Colour the stars.

Return to Page 25 of the Student's Book.

Chapter 3: Create with code 1

Project: Plan a journey for a Bee-Bot to take to tell a story

Chapter 3.1 | **Everyday algorithms**

Task A: Key term algorithm

1 Write your new key term, 'algorithm'.

Key terms

- **algorithm** – set of instructions to complete a task or solve a problem

....

2 Colour your new key term, 'algorithm'.

 Return to Page 28 of the Student's Book.

Task B: Reflection

1 Were any instructions missing from the algorithm to take the class register?

Yes   No

2 Was the algorithm to take the class register in the correct order?

Yes   No

3 Was the algorithm to take the class register easy to understand?

Yes   No

4 Is the order of an algorithm important?

Yes   No

5 Draw a picture of a task where you follow instructions.

Return to Page 29 of the Student's Book.

Task A: Follow a path

Use a pencil to draw the path that the Bee-Bot will take.

Draw the Bee-Bot on the square it will be on after the code has run.

 Tip Remember to draw the Bee-Bot facing the correct direction.

Code:

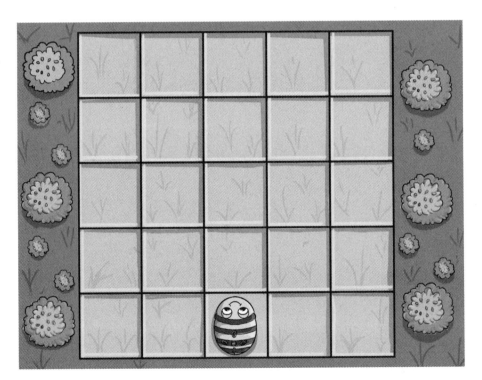

 Return to Page 31 of the Student's Book.

Task B: Create a path

1 Draw a Bee-Bot in one of the squares.

2 Draw a short path for the Bee-Bot to take.

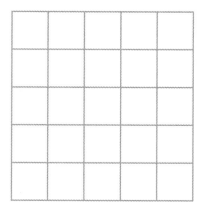

3 Draw the algorithm for the Bee-Bot's path using simple arrows, like in the pictures below.

 Think about the direction the Bee-Bot is facing.

Enter the code for your algorithm on your Bee-Bot by pressing its buttons.

 Return to Page 31 of the Student's Book.

Task A: Label the buttons

1 Draw a line from each label to the correct Bee-Bot button.

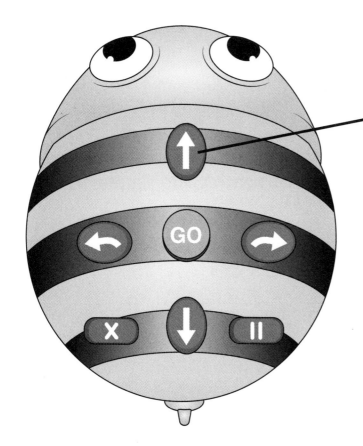

forwards

backwards

run the code

left turn

pause the code

right turn

clear the code

Return to Page 32 of the Student's Book.

Task B: Predict the code: forwards

1 I predict .... presses.

2 Were you correct?   Yes   No

Return to Page 32 of the Student's Book.

Task C: Predict the code: more than one direction

I predict that the code the Bee-Bot needs to reach the object is:

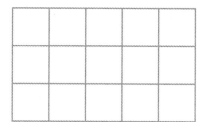

The code the Bee-Bot needed to reach the object was:

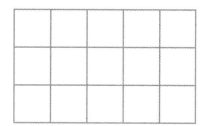

 Return to Page 33 of the Student's Book.

Task D: Reflect

When I made my prediction, I used the information that the forwards button moves a Bee-Bot 15 cm.

Yes   No

When I made my prediction, I used the information that the left and right buttons move a Bee-Bot one quarter turn.

Yes   No

When I made my prediction, I used the information that the left and right buttons turn the Bee-Bot.

Yes   No

Does information help you to make better predictions?

Yes   No

 Return to Page 33 of the Student's Book.

Task A: Plan your story

1 Draw and label the objects you will use in your story.

> **Tip** Look around your classroom for objects that you can use.

2 Write a story for your Bee-Bot to follow. Your story should include all your objects.

....

....

....

....

....

....

Return to Page 35 of the Student's Book.

Task A: Code for your first object

1 My first object is: ....

Write the code to move your Bee-Bot from the starting marker to the first object. You can write the code in the prediction box.

Test and change the route until the Bee-Bot moves to the first object.

```
Prediction box



```

2 Write the final code for your first object by drawing pictures of the buttons.

```
First object code



```

Task B: Code for your second object

1 My second object is: ....

Write the code to move your Bee-Bot from the first object to the second object. You can write the code in the prediction box.

Test and change the route until the Bee-Bot moves to the second object.

> Prediction box

2 Write the final code for your second object.

> Second object code

Task C: Code for your third object

1 My third object is: ....

Write the code to move your Bee-Bot from the second object to the third object. You can write the code in the prediction box.

Test and change the route until the Bee-Bot moves to the third object.

> Prediction box

. Write the final code for your third object.

> Third object code

 Return to Page 36 of the Student's Book.

Task A: Reflection

1 How well did your Bee-Bot tell your story? Colour the stars.

2 How good are you at sharing a story? Colour the stars.

Return to Page 37 of the Student's Book.

Chapter 4: How computers work

○ Project: Make a counting app to help with counting from 1 to 5

Parts of a computer

Task A: Find the inputs

1 Circle the images that are inputs.

mouse

screen

speakers

touchscreen

pencil

keyboard

Key terms

- **computer system** – computer with its connected parts
- **component** – part of a computer system
- **mouse** – component that you move to point to things on a computer screen
- **keyboard** – component that you use to type letters and numbers on a computer
- **screen (or monitor)** – component that shows pictures and videos from a computer
- **printer** – component that can put pictures and words on paper
- **speakers** – component that can play sound from a computer
- **touchpad (or trackpad)** – part of a laptop computer that you use to point to things on a computer screen by moving your finger

Task B: Find the outputs

2 Circle the images that are outputs.

keyboard

touchscreen

speakers

poster

microphone

printer

Key terms

- **touchscreen** – component that shows pictures and videos and allows you to point to things with your finger
- **headphones** – component that can play sound from a computer
- **microphone** – component that can get sound into a computer
- **webcam** – component that can get pictures and video into a computer
- **input** – component that allows a person to enter information into a computer
- **output** – component that presents information to a person

Return to Page 41 of the Student's Book.

Task A: Investigate a Scratch app

Click or tap on the sprites in the app one at a time. What happens when you click on the sprite? Circle the correct answer.

Sprite	What happens when I click the sprite?		
1	A	B	
2	A	B	
3	A	B	
4	A	B	
5	A	B	
6	A	B	

Task B: Which of these inputs did you use?

mouse

1 Circle the inputs that you used.

touchscreen

trackpad

keyboard

Task C: Which of these outputs did you use?

laptop screen

tablet screen

1 Circle the outputs that you used.

monitor

headphones

computer speakers

Return to Page 43 of the Student's Book.

Task A: Try sound effects

1 Circle each sound effect that you try.

Faster Slower Louder Softer Mute Fade in Fade out Reverse Robot

2 Which effect was your favourite?

Faster Slower Louder Softer Mute Fade in Fade out Reverse Robot

 Return to Page 46 of the Student's Book.

Task B: Match the pictures

1 Draw lines to connect each picture to the correct sound effect. The first one has been done for you.

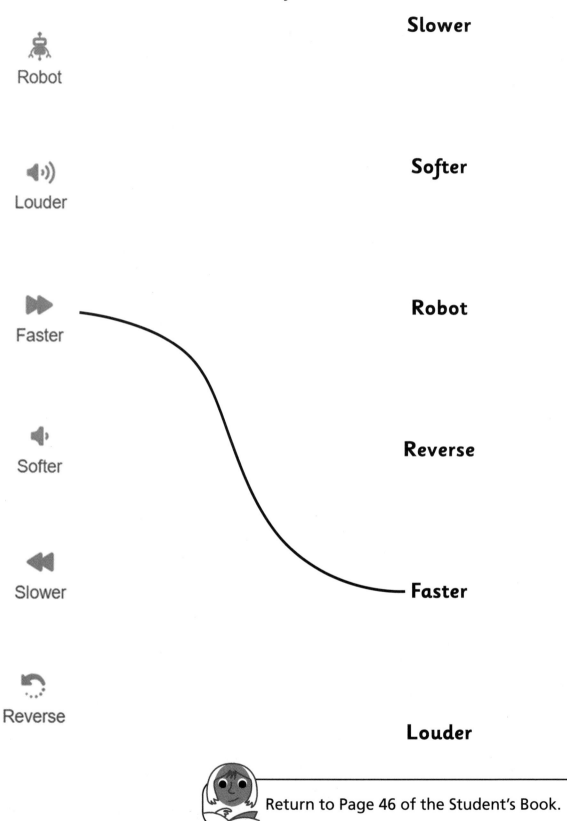

Slower

Robot

Softer

Louder

Robot

Faster

Reverse

Softer

Faster

Slower

Reverse

Louder

Return to Page 46 of the Student's Book.

Task A: Choose costumes for your app

1 Your app will have five sprites. Circle the costume you want to use for each sprite. Choose one costume from each column.

1	2	3	4	5

Return to Page 47 of the Student's Book.

Task A: Record sounds one to five

1 Click on each sprite and make sure they say the correct number.

2 Tick the box ☐ when each sprite says the correct number.

Sprite	Say	Done
1	one	☐
2	two	☐
3	three	☐
4	four	☐
5	five	☐

Task B: Where should you click?

1 Look at the picture. Circle the image where you would click first to record a sound for Sprite 3.

A Middle sprite on the stage (main area with balloons)

B Sounds tab

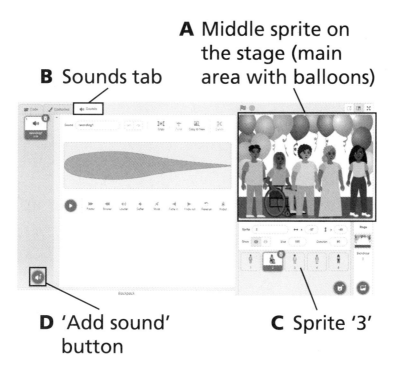

D 'Add sound' button

C Sprite '3'

2 Why is it important to make sure that your work is saved?

....

....

 Return to Page 48 of the Student's Book.

Task A: Reflection

1 How well would your app help children learn to count to 5? Colour the stars.

2 How well did you perform the showcase of your app? Colour the stars.

3 How could you improve your showcase next time?

....

....

Return to Page 49 of the Student's Book.

Chapter 5: Create with code 2

◉ Project: Create a scene with layers to show a view from a window

---

Chapter 5.1 | **Stacking tower**

Task A: Stack the rings

Use the numbers 1 to 5 to give the correct order for stacking the rings. The first one has been done for you.

Key terms

- **code block** – single line of code in Scratch

1

Return to Page 52 of the Student's Book.

Task B: The correct order

1 Click and drag or tap and drag the code blocks into the correct order.

2 Click the green flag when you are ready to test.

3 Keep trying until you get the order right.

4 Draw the code blocks in the correct order in the box below.

Return to Page 53 of the Student's Book.

Task A: Find the error

You can see the code for the sand bucket Scratch project below.

1 Circle the error in the code.

 Tip The order for the colours is: brown, orange, yellow and white.

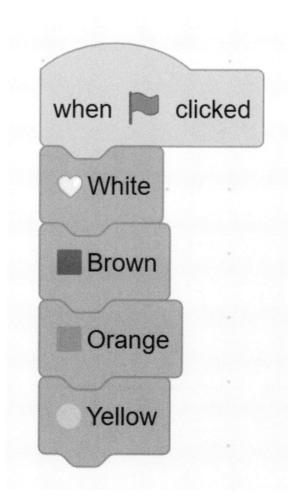

Task B: Fix the error

1 Fix the error in the code.

2 Test it to make sure it works.

3 If it doesn't work, try again.

4 Draw the fixed program in the box below.

Return to Page 55 of the Student's Book.

Task A: Order the layers

1 Create a scene that uses four layers. Use the numbers 1 to 4 to say which order to place the layers. The first one has been done for you.

Layer 1 is the layer furthest away.

 Return to Page 57 of the Student's Book.

Task A: Choose your costumes

1 Circle your favourite window frame.

Brown   Grey   White   Pink   Blue

2 Circle your favourite animal.

3 Circle your favourite tree.

4 Circle your favourite background.

Task B: Order your sprites

The background will be placed first. Write the numbers 2, 3 and 4 in the order that you should place them.

Window frame	
Animal	
Background	1
Trees	

Return to Page 58 of the Student's Book.

Task A: Order the code blocks

Here are the code blocks that you need to run your program.

1 Draw the code blocks in the correct order.

Return to Page 59 of the Student's Book.

Task B: Test your code

1 Click on the green flag 🏳 to see if your program works.

2 Tick the boxes below to check your code:

- I can see the 'Background' sprite ☐

- I can see the 'Tree' sprite ☐

- I can see the 'Animal' sprite ☐

- I can see the 'Window' sprite ☐

3 If you cannot see all your sprites, move your code blocks until you can see all your sprites.

Return to Page 60 of the Student's Book.

Task A: Reflection

1 How easy was it to create your scene app?
Colour the stars.

2 Did your audience like your scene? Colour the stars.

3 How important is it to test and debug projects?
Colour the stars.

Return to Page 61 of the Student's Book.

Chapter 6: Connect the world

◐ Project: Design a webpage on a topic of your choice

| Chapter 6.1 | Wired and wireless connections |

Task A: Connect the computer systems

1 Draw wires to connect the computer systems.

Tip You might have used headphones or a mouse that didn't need wires. For this task they need wires to communicate!

Key terms

- **wired connection** – when devices communicate with each other through a wire
- **wireless connection** – when devices communicate with each other without a wire connecting the devices

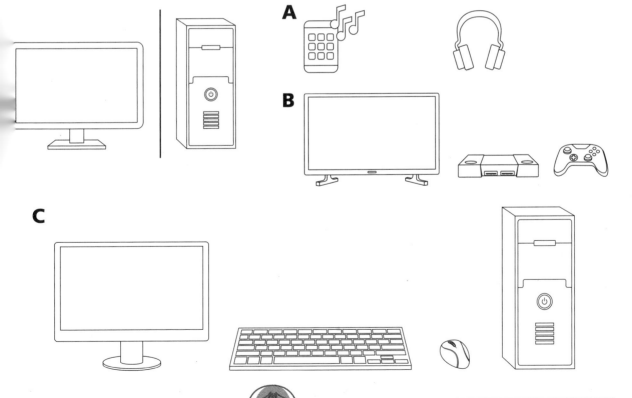

A

B

C

Return to Page 65 of the Student's Book.

Task B: Find the wireless connections

1 Circle the components that are communicating with a wireless connection.

A

B

C

Return to Page 65 of the Student's Book.

Task A: Connect to the printer

1 Draw wires to connect all the computers in the network so that they can communicate with the printer.

Return to Page 66 of the Student's Book.

Task B: Send a message

1 Draw arrows to show how the message can get from Computer 1 to Computer 2.

The message can only move along the lines.

The first arrow has been drawn for you.

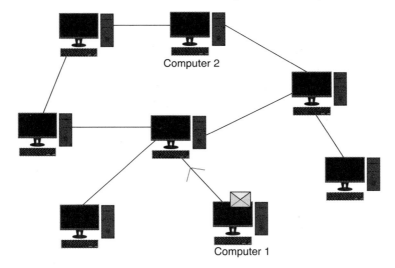

Computer 2

Computer 1

Return to Page 67 of the Student's Book.

Task C: Connecting to the internet

1 Can a tablet connect to the internet?

Yes   No

2 Can a laptop connect to the internet?

Yes   No

3 Can a smartphone connect to the internet?

Yes   No

4 Is the internet always available?

Yes   No

Return to Page 67 of the Student's Book.

Task A: Fill in the letters

1 Fill in the missing letters.

A The ....orld ....ide ....eb is all the webpages on the internet.

B A we....s....te is a collection of web ....ages.

C A w....bpa....e is a document that your computer gets from the internet.

Return to Page 68 of the Student's Book.

Task B: Staying safe

1 How can you stay safe on a computer? Fill in the missing words.

A

.... a grown-up if you want to use a computer.

B

.... a grown-up if you see something on the computer that worries you.

Return to Page 69 of the Student's Book.

Key terms

- **webpage** – document that your computer gets from the internet
- **website** – collection of webpages
- **World Wide Web (WWW)** – all the webpages on the internet

Task A: Choose a topic

1 Choose a topic for your webpage. It could be about your hobby, your favourite recipe or your favourite place. Or it can be about anything else you choose!

2 Write your topic in the box.

....

....

....

 Return to Page 71 of the Student's Book.

Task B: What is on a webpage?

1 Draw lines from the labels to the correct part of the webpage.

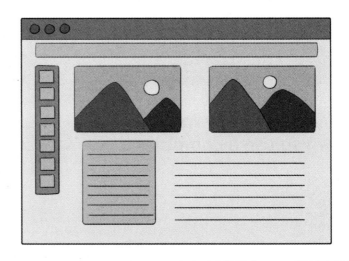

| Buttons | Writing | Pictures | Heading |

Task C: Plan your webpage

1 Sketch your webpage.
Remember to:

- add a heading

- draw shapes for images

- add squiggles for words.

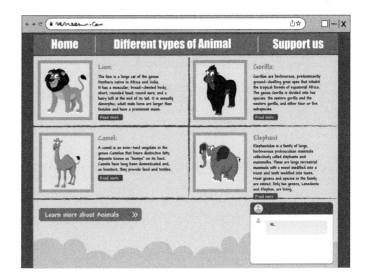

Return to Page 71 of the Student's Book.

Task A: Age of webpage visitors

1 What age children is your webpage for? Circle the ages.

3   4   5   6

2 Why did you choose this age group?

....

....

 Return to Page 72 of the Student's Book.

Task B: Design your webpage

1 Use this space for ideas and notes.

You should think about:

- things visitors your age would like to see

- ideas from your teacher about your webpage plan.

Tip You could:
- use coloured pencils to show your colours
- write your heading
- practise drawing the webpage pictures.

2 Draw and write your finished design here.

 Return to Page 72 of the Student's Book.

Task A: Reflection

1 How much would children like your webpage? Colour the stars.

2 How well did you perform the showcase of your design? Colour the stars.

3 What did you do well in your showcase?

....

....

What could you do better in your next showcase?

....

....

Return to Page 73 of the Student's Book.

61

Chapter 7: The power of data

◑ Project: Plan a dream class celebration

Task A: Search safely

1 What should you do if you see something online that makes you feel worried, scared or sad? Tick the correct answer.

Key terms

- **search engine** – app that can be used to find information from the internet
- **form** – document that helps you collect answers to more than one question

A  Click on it.

B  Show a friend.

C  Tell a grown up.

Return to Page 76 of the Student's Book.

Task B: Fill in the form

A form helps you to collect answers to more than one question. Fill in this form.

All about you:

1 Do you like snakes?

Yes   No

2 Have you used a Bee-Bot?

Yes   No

3 What is your favourite colour?

....

Return to Page 77 of the Student's Book.

Task C: Reflect

1 When would you use a search engine?

A To ask more than one question at the same time

B To find answers from websites on the internet

When would you use a tally chart?

A To collect answers from more than one person

B To find answers from websites on the internet

When would you use a form?

A To ask more than one question at the same time

B To find answers from websites on the internet

Return to Page 77 of the Student's Book.

Task A: Count the tigers

1 How many tigers are there in this picture?

....

2 How many tigers are there in this picture?

....

Return to Page 79 of the Student's Book.

Task B: Count the insects

1 How many bees are there in this picture?

....

2 Are there more ants or ladybirds in this picture?

....

3 How many ants are there in this picture?

....

4 Are there more bees or beetles in this picture?

....

5 How many beetles are there in this picture?

....

6 Are there more bees or ladybirds in this picture?

....

Return to Page 79 of the Student's Book.

Task A: My class celebration

1 Draw a picture of how you would like to celebrate. You could draw food, drinks, decorations and games or activities.

Return to Page 80 of the Student's Book.

Task B: Our class form

1 Make a form to help plan your class celebration.

Write down the questions that you agree as a class.

1 ....

2 ....

3 ....

Return to Page 81 of the Student's Book.

Task A: Online form checklist

☐ I have opened the online form.

☐ I have answered question 1.

☐ I have answered question 2.

☐ I have answered question 3.

☐ I have sent my answers.

Key terms

• **online form** – webpage with questions for people to answer

Return to Page 83 of the Student's Book.

Task B: My prediction

1 What do you think the most popular answer will be for each question? The most popular answer is the one chosen by the greatest number of people.

Question 1: ....

Question 2: ....

Question 3: ....

Return to Page 83 of the Student's Book.

Task A: Sort the tables

1 Write your answers in the table.

   A What is the most popular hobby?

   B What is the second most popular hobby?

   C What is the least popular hobby?

Favourite hobbies		
Hobby	**Number of people**	Most popular **A** ....
reading	II	**B** ....
sports	III	**C** ....
art	꒢꒢꒢꒢꒢	Least popular

2 Write your answers in the table.

   A What is the most popular colour?

   B What is the second most popular colour?

   C What is the least popular colour?

Favourite colours		
Colour	**Number of people**	Most popular **A** ....
red	3	**B** ....
blue	5	**C** ....
pink	4	Least popular

3 Write your answers in the table.

    A What is the most popular fruit?

    B What is the second most popular fruit?

    C What is the least popular fruit?

Favourite fruit		
Fruit	**Number of people**	Most popular A ....
melon		B ....
grapes		C ....
apple		Least popular

Return to Page 84 of the Student's Book.

Task B: Popular choices

Your teacher will share your class celebration data with you.

1 What was the most popular answer to each question?

Question 1: ....

Question 2: ....

Question 3: ....

Return to Page 84 of the Student's Book.

Task A: Our class celebration

1 Draw a picture of how your class chose to celebrate. Remember to draw the food, the drinks and what you did.

Return to Page 85 of the Student's Book.

Task B: Reflection

1 Did everyone in the class help plan the celebration? Colour the stars.

2 How good are you at answering questions with data? Colour the stars.

3 Draw something that was included in your celebration because of the data you collected.

Return to Page 85 of the Student's Book.